Turtle Light Press Haiku Chapbook Contest Winners

Furrows of Snow, Glenn G. Coats (2019)

The Deep End of the Sky, Chad Lee Robinson (2015)

The Window That Closes, Graham High (2013)

All That Remains, Catherine J.S. Lee (2011)

Sketches from the San Joaquin, Michael McClintock (2009)

Other Turtle Light Press Haiku Books

Nick Virgilio: A Life in Haiku, Nick Virgilio
(Edited by Raffael de Gruttola)

Peace and War: A Collection of Haiku from Israel, Rick Black

Also by Glenn G. Coats

Adult Literacy

Waiting for the Sky, 2014

One Small Field of Corn, 2015

Children's

When Miss Parson Forgot Halloween, 2018

Waiting for a Frog, 1997

Haiku

Naming the Boulders, 2009

Haibun

Degrees of Acquaintance, 2019 (e-book)

waking and dream, 2017

Beyond the Muted Trees, 2014

Snow on the Lake, 2013

Memoir

An Innocent Mission, 2015

Trying to Move Mountains, 2004

☙

Furrows of Snow

Furrows of Snow

Glenn G. Coats

Turtle Light Press • Arlington, Va. • 2019

2019 Turtle Light Press Trade Paperback Edition

Copyright © 2019 by Glenn G. Coats

Published in the United States by Turtle Light Press, LLC

All rights reserved. No part of this book may be used or reproduced without written permission except in the case of brief quotations embodied in critical articles and reviews. To print or reproduce individual poems, please contact Glenn G. Coats at his email: glenn.coats5@gmail.com For all other inquiries, please contact Turtle Light Press at this email: rick@turtlelightpress.com

ISBN 978-0-9748147-6-6

First Edition

Book cover and interior design by Rick Black and Emma Cortellessa

The front cover is a photo montage of the author's mother, Rachel Coats; ice fishing in Finland by Heather Sunderland used under a Creative Commons license; and a map of New Jersey from www.nationalmap.gov.

Turtle Light Press
P.O. Box 50162
Arlington, VA 22205
U.S.A.

www.turtlelightpress.com
rick@turtlelightpress.com

*For my daughter,
Caitlin Ann McMullen,
who also sings rivers*

Sunday sermons
rivers that bend
my knees

summer currents
I speak more slowly
to my mother

night sky
I release the minnows
all at once

campfire light
a stretch of song
along the river

wind in the brush
riverbeds crack
like shells

hum of mosquitoes
        one last cast
                at the moon

winter shadows
I try to tell my mother
who I am

ragged shoreline
the ground not as true
as it once was

a whistle
to call her back
river mist

a circle of boots
around the deepest hole
river dawn

loneliness rises
    to the surface
        autumn hideaway

leaden sky
I clap the river
from my hands

barn light
a rush of creeks
to the river

rippled water
I see mother's cursive
in mine

morning tide
the sand swept clean
of stories

mouth of the river
I dream with my cousin
boat to boat

rocky shoreline
my daughter guides a fish
into my hands

summer of fishing
a permanent bend
in the cane pole

wind-bent pines
mother stands straight
as she can

midnight snow
the lullaby repeats
again and again

quiet prayers
fish gather at the mouths
of creeks

seventy springs
    the time it takes
        to know the river

rain on the marsh
   swollen fingers
      find the chords

she asks
would I know them now?
violets

Furrows of snow

melting snow
songs that are gone
by morning

river stones
mother slips a step
further away

alone on the water
I hang on to what's left
of the light

furrows of snow
the river threads a way
to the sea

winter hawks
　　mother's silence
　　　　follows me home

The Back Story

Rivers have always been a big part of my life. In New Jersey, my grandfather had a summer cottage on the Toms River and Barnegat Bay and I spent a lot of time with him. By the time I was 15, I had my own rowboat with a motor on it. It was very inspiring for me; I always loved being on the water.

I was always fishing—the south branch of the Raritan, the Delaware River, the Musconetcong and the Pequest. I remember after I was teaching in Flemington, N.J., I was at a park along the water and a fisherman came up to me and said, "Is that your blue truck? Whenever I see that blue truck, it's parked near water." As I got older, I focused more on streams and fly fishing—and now I'm back to a river, the Intracoastal Waterway.

Rivers have always been a part of my writing. I feel at home by a river. I like studying the tides and knowing that an incoming tide is going to wash the minnows up the brackish creeks and an outgoing tide is going to pull the baitfish back to the shallows of the creek, and I can drift in my boat at the mouth of the creek. I throw them all back, anyway.

I do feel a comfort on the water. I forget my age when I'm on the water—and even when my back hurts. I also think water is a connection between my grandfather, my father and my son; it's a connection that we had between us.

In writing *Furrows of Snow*, I had in mind that my mother—like the river—is the source of my being here and a source of finding peace and comfort in my life. Several poems were written by the Schuylkill but I was thinking about rivers, of different rivers. I was waiting for my granddaughter to be born.

I would write a poem about a river on a post-it note, date it and put it in my wallet. Eventually I took them out and wrote them all down and when I looked at them, I began to look at other haiku about rivers, too. I laid them all out and read them over and over. I kept reading and rereading, and if it wasn't right, I took it out. I wanted to find that balance between river poems and the poems about my mother.

About the Author

Glenn G. Coats was born in 1950 in Rahway, New Jersey. He spent a lot of his youth fishing on the Toms River and Barnegat Bay. He fondly remembers going out fishing with his father or grandfather, and bringing home the day's catch.

For 34 years, Coats worked as a reading teacher in elementary schools in Flemington, N.J. He specialized in working with children who were having a hard time learning to read. Afterwards, Coats moved to Farmville, VA, where he taught adult literacy as well as English as a second language at Longwood University.

He has been writing haiku for more than 30 years and got started the way a lot of elementary school teachers do—by teaching haiku as a creative writing lesson. He then got into it more seriously himself, reading extensively, writing poems and submitting to journals.

"I like cutting things down to the heart of a poem," he says. "I love the brevity of haiku. I really love when a haiku can even tell a story. I can read someone's haiku and imagine a whole story, not just a flash of an image."

Over the years, Coats has won numerous awards, including a 2018 Merit Book Award from the Haiku Society of America, first place in the Peggy Willis Lyles contest, first place for the Lyman Haiku Award from the North Carolina Poetry Society, and many others. He has also been published in journals around the world. He is a three-time Pushcart nominee and served as co-editor at *Haibun Today*.

He is now retired and lives with his wife, Joani, in Carolina Shores, North Carolina, where he loves to explore the Intracoastal Waterway with one of his six grandchildren.

Acknowledgments

I am grateful to the editors of the following publications and contests where many of these poems, or versions of them, first appeared:

Acorn, bottle rockets, Contemporary Haibun Online, Frogpond, Haibun Today, The Haiku Calendar 2017, The Haiku Society of America Anthology 2018, The Heron's Nest, The Heron's Nest - They Gave Us Life Anthology, The Irish Haiku Society Competition 2014, The Sacred in Contemporary Haiku.

Special thanks to the many editors and writers who have helped to shape my work, especially Menke Katz who helped me see the essence (bare bones) of a poem, Peggy Lyles and Stanford Forrester for sharing their haiku expertise, as well as Jeffrey Woodward, Ray Rasmussen, and Richard Straw for encouraging me to write haibun.

All of their voices are behind the words in this book.

November 2019
Carolina Shores, North Carolina

Colophon

The body of this book and poems are set in Goudy Old Style. The cover and title page font is Futura Light.

Photo on the title page is reproduced courtesy of Sigfrid Lundberg under a Creative Commons license. The photo on page 28 is reproduced courtesy of Jessica Bolser under a Creative Commons license, too.

The other photos used in the book have been provided by the author and appear as follows:

- Glenn G. Coats wading on the Pequest River
- Cordgrass
- Fragment of Rachel Coats's handwriting
- Caitlin, the author's daughter, with a fish on Indian Lake
- Rachel Coats, the author's mother

Our grateful thanks to Susan Antolin who served as judge of this haiku chapbook competition.

www.ingramcontent.com/pod-product-compliance
Lightning Source LLC
Chambersburg PA
CBHW051718040426
42446CB00008B/944